GOOD
HOUSEKEEPING
LOOK
and
COOK

GOOD HOUSEKEEPING
LOOK and COOK

A Picture Guide to Cooking Skills

Compiled by
The Good Housekeeping
Institute

Illustrated by
Julia Fryer

EBURY PRESS
LONDON

Published by Ebury Press
Chestergate House
Vauxhall Bridge Road
London SW1V 1HF

First impression 1978

ISBN 0 85223 135 0   **80428**

Compiled by Barbara Argles
Designer Derek Morrison
Cookery Adviser Margaret Coombes
Jacket design by Ivan Ripley

Filmset and printed by
BAS Printers Limited, Over Wallop, Hampshire
Bound by Ebenezer Baylis & Son Limited, Worcester

Foreword

Have you ever got half way through a recipe only to find that you've no idea how to bind ingredients together, bard the bird, bake blind or even how to tell if the stew is cooking correctly? All these mysteries and many more are explained in detail – in words and pictures – in this book.

No aspiring cook can afford to be without this dictionary of cooking skills. It is set out alphabetically for easy reference. The line drawings illustrating each skill show you exactly what to do.

Look and Cook has been compiled by the Good Housekeeping Institute experts. It's a book to keep handy in the kitchen but if you have any queries we can bring over 50 years of experience to your aid: Write to Good Housekeeping Institute, Chestergate House, Vauxhall Bridge Road, London SW1V 1HF for a personal reply.

GOOD HOUSEKEEPING INSTITUTE

Useful cookery information

Handy list of kitchen equipment used in the book

FOR COOKING AND STORING

Saucepans in assorted sizes
Milk saucepan
Dariole moulds
Steamer
Asparagus steamer
Frying pan
Omelette pan
Sauté pan
Preserving pan
Deep fat fryer
Egg poacher
Colander
Electric or ordinary kettle
Roasting tins

Baking sheet
Sandwich tins
Cake tins in assorted sizes
Swiss roll tin
Loaf tin
Bun trays
Wire cooling rack
Mixing bowl
Pudding basins
Measuring jug (marked
    metric and imperial)
Ovenproof plates
Pie dishes
Casseroles

Ramekin dishes
Flan ring
Jelly mould
Raised pie mould
Dariole moulds
Ring mould
Soufflé dish
Roaster bags
Storage jars and tins
Polythene storage boxes
Electric mixer or blender
    and attachments
Spit roast
Bottling jars, rings, etc.

TOOLS AND UTENSILS

Kitchen knives
Wooden spoons
Perforated frying spoon
Fish slice
Pastry cutters
Skewers
Set of metric measuring
    spoons
A pair of scales (marked
    metric and imperial)
Rolling pin
Pastry board
Pastry brush
Chopping board
    (melamine type)
Potato peeler
Apple corer
A pair of kitchen scissors
Can opener
Balloon whisk
Mouli grater
Lemon squeezer

Sieves
Mincing machine
Nut cracker
Cook's thermometer
Meat thermometer
Flat whisk
Grapefruit knife
Butter pat
Zester
Drainer
Egg slicer
Steaming/mesh basket
Meat hammer
Food mill
Egg separator
Freezer pump
Pepper mill
Hopper
Weights
Meat press
Ladle
Garlic press

Tongs
Wooden spatula
Pestle and mortar
Coffee grinder
Cherry stoner
Jelly bag and stand
Pincers
Chining saw
Carving knife and fork
Kitchen timer
Onion chopper
Curved chopper and bowl
Palette knife
Poultry shears
Larding needle
Dredger
Icing bags and assorted
    nozzles
Piping bags and nozzles
Icing turntable
Icing ruler
Icing comb

Roasting guide

BEEF
Cook top quality joints at 220°C (425°F) mark 7 for 15–20 minutes per 0·5 kg (1 lb) plus 15–20 minutes over, depending on rareness. For less good quality joints cook at 190°C (375°F) mark 5 for 25 minutes per 0·5 kg (1 lb) (boned and rolled 30 minutes). Cheap roasting cuts are best cooked at 170°C–180°C (325°F–350°F) mark 3–4 for 40 minutes per 0·5 kg (1 lb).

LAMB
Cook joints with bone at 180°C (350°F) mark 4 for 27 minutes per 0·5 kg (1 lb) plus 27 minutes over.

PORK
Cook at 190°C (375°F) mark 5 for 30 minutes per 0·5 kg (1 lb) plus 30 minutes over.

VEAL
Cook at 220°C (425°F) mark 7 for 25 minutes per 0·5 kg (1 lb) plus 25 minutes over. Baste or cover with bacon.

CHICKEN
A 1·8-kg (4-lb) oven-ready chicken serves 4–5. Cook without foil at 190°C (375°F) mark 5 for 20 minutes per 0·5 kg (1 lb) plus 20 minutes over. Times vary slightly depending on ratio of bone and tightness of trussing.

Beurre manié Equal quantities of butter and flour blended together to a paste (see page 89).

Bouquet garni A small bunch of herbs tied together in muslin and used to give flavour to stews and casseroles. A simple bouquet garni consists of a sprig of parsley and thyme, a bay leaf, 2 cloves and a few peppercorns (see page 20).

Seasoned flour Used for dusting meat, fish etc. before frying or stewing. Mix about 30 ml (2 level tbsp) flour with about 5 ml (1 level tsp) salt and a good sprinkling of pepper (see page 90).

Aspic

To coat cold foods – to set them in a mould or to hold garnishes in place – with a clear savoury jelly made from the appropriate juices of cooked meat, poultry or fish. Aspic can also be chopped and used as a garnish.

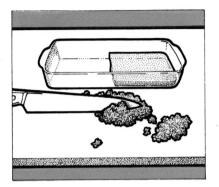

Chopping set aspic jelly roughly with a knife blade to use it for garnishing a cold dish. Wet the knife blade to prevent the jelly sticking and always work on a damp surface.

Bake

To cook by dry heat in the oven. As well as cakes, pastries, bread and biscuits, meat, fish, eggs, some vegetables and fruit can also be baked.

Baking two sandwich cakes in a pre-heated oven. Place the tins on the same shelf and stagger them to ensure even heat distribution, leaving a space between the oven walls and tins and the tins themselves.

Bake blind

To bake flan cases, tarts and tartlet pastry cases without a filling. The pastry may be lined with greaseproof paper and dried beans, foil, or small tartlet cases just pricked with a fork.

1

Pressing the pastry dough into the fluted ridges of the flan dish. Trim the edges. Cut a round of greaseproof paper slightly larger than the pastry case and use to line.

2

Weighing down with dried beans to prevent the pastry from rising as it bakes. Remove the beans and paper 5–10 minutes before the end of cooking time. Save the beans to use again.

Bard

To cover lean meat or the breast of poultry or game birds with slices or offcuts of fat bacon rashers, trimmings or pork fat before roasting, to prevent the flesh from drying out. The bacon bastes the lean meat.

Placing the streaky bacon rashers evenly over the breast of a pheasant and securing with string. About 10 minutes before the end of the cooking time, remove the bacon.

Baste

To ladle hot fat or liquid over food being roasted or baked, in order to keep it moist and to improve both the flavour and appearance. A long-handled spoon or a special basting bulb can be used.

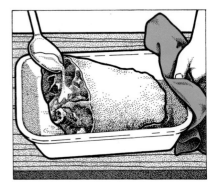

Spooning the hot pan juices over a joint of meat to keep it succulent. Basting should be done frequently during the roasting time.

Bat

To flatten slices of raw meat, usually escalopes, by beating with a rolling pin or a meat bat before cooking. It is also helpful in tenderising steaks of doubtful quality by breaking down the tissues.

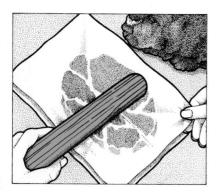

Beating an escalope of veal, placed between two pieces of waxed or non-stick paper, evenly with a rolling pin. The meat should be beaten firmly until it is about 0.5 cm (¼ in) thick.

Beat

To agitate an ingredient, such as eggs, or mixture – sauce or batter – to incorporate air and make it light and smooth. Beating can be done with a wooden spoon, flat spatula, fork, whisk or electric mixer.

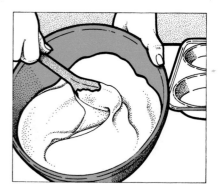

Using a wooden spoon to beat air into a Yorkshire pudding batter. Work vigorously turning the mixture over and over.

Bind

To add a moist substance like cream, egg or melted fat to dry ingredients to hold them together in a soft mixture. For instance, a thick white sauce is used in a fish croquette mixture to bind the fish together.

Using a fork to mix an egg into the dry ingredients for a forcemeat stuffing. There is no need to beat the egg first provided it is evenly worked into the mixture.

Blanch

To treat food with boiling water in order to whiten it; to preserve its natural colour; to loosen its skin; to remove any strong or bitter taste; to kill unwanted enzymes before freezing or preserving.

1

Preparing fresh green beans for the freezer. Put them in a wire basket and lower into a pan of boiling water. Bring back to the boil quickly and blanch for 3 minutes.

2

Plunging the basket of blanched beans into a bowl of iced water to cool them quickly, preventing further cooking.

Loosening the skins of almonds by pouring over boiling water. Allow to stand for 2–3 minutes. Add cold water to the bowl before rubbing off the skins between the fingers. Dry.

Blend

To combine ingredients evenly using a spoon, spatula or knife. To thicken soups, stews etc, flour is blended with cold water, milk or stock before boiling liquid is added. This prevents lumps from forming. Also applies to an electric blender.

Mixing cold milk into custard powder and sugar with a wooden spatula. When thoroughly blended, add the measured amount of boiling milk, return to the boil to obtain a thick lump-free sauce.

Boil

To cook in liquid – water, stock, milk – at a minimum of 100°C (212°F) at which temperature the surface of the liquid will be broken continuously by bubbles.

Adding salt to the boiling water in which shredded cabbage is about to be cooked. Note that the water barely covers the vegetables so that loss of flavour and food value is minimised. Cover with the lid. (See SHRED.)

Boiling an egg, gently. Vigorous boiling, as shown left, will spoil the eating quality and may crack the shell. Adjust the heat so the surface of the water just trembles, see right.

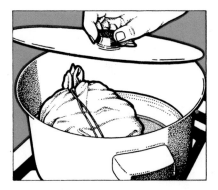

Putting the lid on a large pan containing a suet pudding, wrapped in a cloth. The pudding is added to gently boiling water. Top up with boiling water during cooking time.

Bone

To remove bones from meat, poultry, game or fish before cooking. This is done to make eating, carving and/or stuffing easier.

1

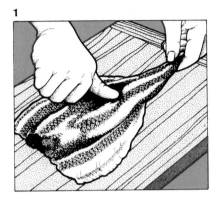

Running a thumb firmly down the back of a herring to loosen the bone. Place the split and gutted herring, skin side upwards, on a board to do this.

2

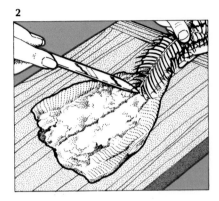

Pulling the backbone out, having turned the fish over. Start pulling at the head end and use a knife to ease the backbone out, if necessary.

1

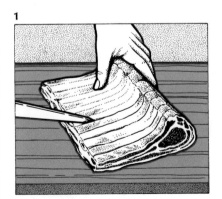

Cutting between the rib bones of a best end of lamb. Cut with a sharp kitchen knife the full length and depth of the bone. The joint should first be chined (See CHINE).

2

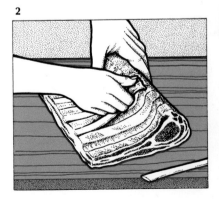

Easing the rib bones, one by one, away from the flesh. Use a knife to help loosen the flesh then pull away each bone with the hand. The joint can then be stuffed and/or rolled. ➡

1

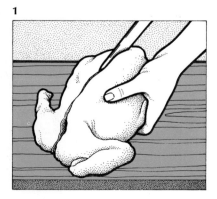

Making a cut down the centre of the back of a chicken with a small sharp knife. Start at the neck end, having first removed the wing tips.

2

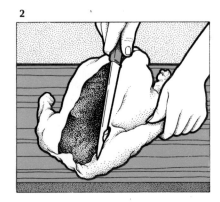

Nicking the sinews at the wing joint after carefully cutting the flesh away from the rib cage, down to the wing joint. By scraping, carefully remove the wing bone. Repeat this procedure for the other wing joint.

3

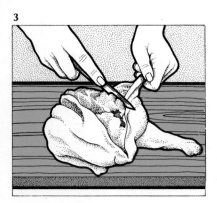

Cutting the flesh away from the carcass to reveal the leg joint. Scrape the flesh from the thigh bone and ease the bone out.

4

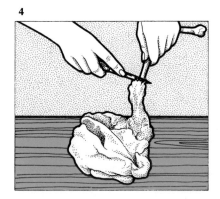

Scraping the flesh from the drumstick, nicking sinews at the joint. Pull the bone from the flesh turning it inside out. Repeat this procedure for the other leg.

Braise

To cook meat, poultry, game or fish slowly in the oven or on top of the cooker in a covered pot on a bed of sliced or diced vegetables. Root vegetables can also be braised on their own. Braising helps tenderise and flavour tougher meat.

Preparing meat for braising. After browning in hot fat, place the meat on a bed of sliced root vegetables. Add just enough liquid to keep the meat moist. Seal tightly with a well fitting lid.

Brand

To scorch or burn the surface of a finished dish or steak with a hot skewer for a decorative effect.

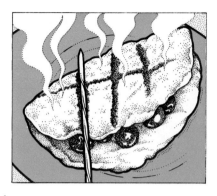

Branding the top of a sweet omelette. Sprinkle the omelette with icing sugar. Hold a metal skewer in an oven cloth, heat the other end over a flame, then lay it across the icing sugar.

Brine

To preserve or pickle food, usually meat or vegetables, by immersing in a salt solution or by treating with a dry salt mixture.

1

Rubbing a dry mixture of salt, sugar, saltpetre, peppercorns, juniper berries, bay leaves and thyme into the skin side of a piece of belly pork, working vigorously. Turn the pork over and repeat more lightly.

2

Placing the belly pork, fat side up, on a bed of seasoned dry salt mixture in a glass bowl. Pack more mixture round the side and over the top. Cover with a wooden board and weight, and leave in the dry brine at least five days. ➡

Brine *continued*

Straining brine solution containing salt-petre, salt and juniper berries tied in muslin on to meat in a crock for wet brining. Keep the meat immersed by placing a clean plate and weight over it.

Caramelise To heat
sugar slowly until it turns liquid and goes brown. Alternatively, sugar can be dissolved by stirring in hot water and left over heat until it gently boils and turns brown. Caramelised sugar is used for flavouring.

Pouring caramelised sugar into a buttered soufflé dish to coat the bottom in preparation for a crème caramel. Pour some more on to a marble slab or clean greased baking sheet, allow to set and then break it up for decoration.

Carve To slice cooked meat, hot
or cold, into pieces for serving, using a sharp carving knife of suitable shape. A carving fork has a finger guard to protect the hand should the knife slip.

1

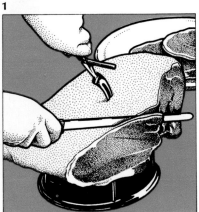

Slicing gammon, cooked on the bone, from the side or 'slipper' area. Place the joint on a spiked holder. Slice as shown to the bone using a long, round ended ham knife.

2

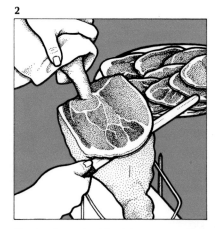

Carving the underside of the gammon. Roll the meat over to do this after the middle and 'slipper' meat has been carved and the knee and aitchbone removed.

Carve *continued*

1

Loosening beef from the wing ribs, after the chine bone at the thick end of the joint has been removed. Use a sharp carving knife with a curve at the pointed end.

2

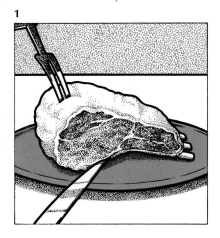

Carving the beef thinly in downward slices which will come away easily from the ribs.

1

Carving a sirloin of beef on the bone by inserting a sharp carving knife between the meat and the bone to loosen it before starting to slice.

2

Slicing the top side of the beef thinly. When this is finished, remove the bone and carve the remaining meat.

1

Removing a section of crackling from a pork loin joint (previously chined) to make it easier to carve.

2

Cutting the pork, with crackling removed, at a slight angle and a little thicker than beef. Serve each portion with a piece of crackling.

1

Carving a shoulder of lamb. Start with the crisp skin uppermost and cut 0.5-cm (¼-in) slices from the thick part of the joint as shown.

2

Cutting the rest of the lamb meat from the top side of the joint before turning it over to carve the underside in horizontal slices.

1

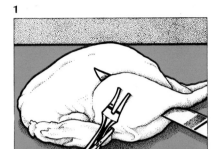

Taking a drumstick and thigh off a turkey by cutting between leg and breast down to the joint. It may be easier to hold the end of the leg than to use a fork.

2

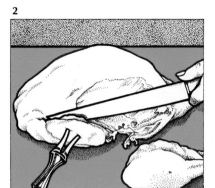

Cutting through the wing joint to remove it before carving the breast meat.

3

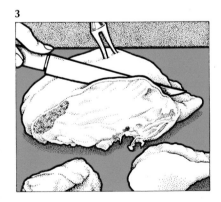

Carving the breast in thin even slices. Start each subsequent slice a little higher up on the breast.

4

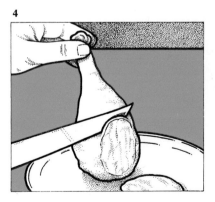

Slicing the meat from the turkey leg. A knife for carving poultry usually has a shorter and more curved blade than one for joints of meat.

Casserole

To cook meat, poultry and/or vegetables with liquid and seasoning very slowly in a tightly lidded cooking pot or casserole dish. Cooking this way tenderises tougher meats and develops a full flavour.

Adding stock to cubed meat, prepared vegetables and bouquet garni (see page 7) in a casserole dish before covering and cooking slowly in the oven. Serve straight from the same dish if wished.

Chine

To separate the backbone from the ribs in a joint of meat before cooking. Loin and neck of lamb, pork or veal are best prepared this way so they can be carved more easily into chops or cutlets.

Using a saw to sever the rib bones from the back bone while holding the joint firmly on a chopping board. A butcher will often do this for you.

Chop

To cut food into very small pieces with a sharp kitchen knife or special chopper. Always chop on a surface that will not be damaged by sharp blades or damage the blades themselves.

Chopping an onion with a special gadget which has sprung blades within an outer casing that prevents both the pieces from scattering and the pungent vapour from escaping. Place the onion cut surface down to prevent slipping.

Using a kitchen knife to chop a halved and sliced onion. Chop holding the pointed tip of the knife in one place to act as a pivot, moving the handle up and down and working round in a semi circle.

Chopping parsley with a fairly large cook's knife on a chopping board. Hold the pointed tip steady in one position to act as a pivot and move the handle up and down, working across the herb in a semi circle.

Using a curved chopper in a wooden bowl to chop herbs and nuts. This method prevents the ingredients scattering.

Clarify To clear or purify fat
which has been used for roasting or frying, by removing any water, salt or meat juices. Also to remove water and salt from butter or margarine and to clear consommés and jellies.

Straining melted butter through muslin to clarify it. Heat the butter gently, without browning, until any water is driven off (it will cease to bubble). Leave to stand before straining.

Scraping the sediment off clarified dripping. Melt the dripping and pour over it twice its quantity of boiling water. Stir and pour into a basin. The fat will rise and the sediment sink. When set, scrape off the sediment.

Coat

To cover foods with batter, crumbs or flour to form a protective coating before frying; to coat cakes for decoration; to mask food with a sauce.

Rolling a sponge cake over chopped nuts to cover the sides. First spread butter cream or jam on the sides so that the nuts will stick. Ice the top of the cake last.

Testing the consistency of a coating sauce by dipping a wooden spoon into the pan. Hold the spoon sideways to see if the sauce forms a thin coat over it. This is the test for a glacé icing too.

Dipping a floured fillet of fish into a batter of coating consistency before frying it in deep fat.

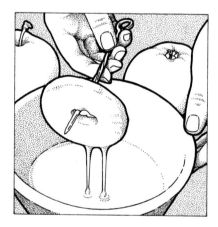

Using a skewer to dip an apple ring into fritter batter (which fries crisply) to ensure an even coating of the batter.

Coat *continued*

Spooning mayonnaise over hard-boiled eggs to make an attractive individual starter salad with tomato.

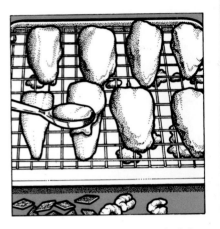

Spooning a chaudfroid sauce, which has just reached setting point, over cold cooked sole fillets or chicken breasts on a wire tray. Garnish and leave to set.

1

Brushing a fillet of fish with lightly beaten egg before coating in breadcrumbs. Use a pastry brush to ensure the egg covers the whole surface.

2

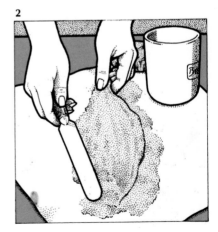

Spreading the fine breadcrumbs on the egg-covered fish, using a palette knife to press the crumbs firmly and evenly on to the fish so that it is well protected while frying.

Core
To remove the hard, indigestible centre of certain foods, particularly fruits such as apples, pears and pineapples. The term is also used to describe removing the centre of kidneys.

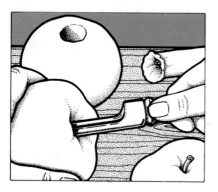

Removing the core from a whole apple with a special coring implement. Push the corer down into the apple from the stem end, twist and pull out the core leaving the apple intact.

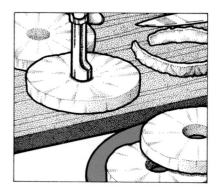

Using the same corer to extract the hard centre from skinned slices of fresh pineapple. This can also be done with a small plain biscuit cutter or the end of a vegetable piping nozzle.

1

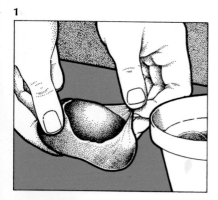

Peeling away the thin transparent skin which surrounds a kidney. Slice the kidney lengthways with a sharp knife to expose the central core.

2

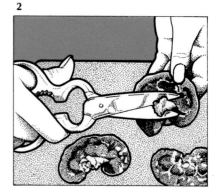

Snipping out the firm core with a pair of kitchen scissors. Alternatively, leave kidney whole and, using scissors, carefully snip round the core to release.

Cream

To beat together fat and sugar until it resembles whipped cream in colour and texture, in other words, pale and fluffy. This method of mixing is used for cakes and puddings with a high proportion of fat.

Creaming fat and sugar in a bowl placed on a cloth to prevent it slipping. Press the back of the spoon against the bowl to help break down the sugar granules. If the fat is too firm beat it alone before adding the sugar.

Crimp

To finish the edge of a double layer of pastry with fluted curves; to cut cucumber and other vegetables so that slices have a deckled edge; or to cut through the flesh of fish so the heat penetrates during cooking.

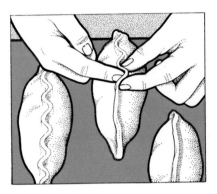

Finishing pasties with a crimped edge by pinching the edges of the pastry together and then with the fingers making flutes along the top.

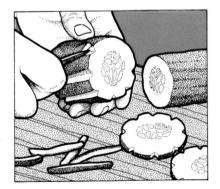

Cutting out long narrow strips from the skin of a cucumber to give the slices a decorative edge. Use a small sharp pointed knife. Cucumber may also be crimped using a fork (See GARNISH).

Scoring both sides of a herring or mackerel with a sharp knife before grilling. The cuts, about 2·5 cm (1 in) apart, help the heat to penetrate quickly and evenly.

Crush

To break down food into smaller particles either, as in the case of spices or garlic, to release the flavour in cooking or to make a crumb-like texture, as with biscuits, for mixing with other ingredients.

Pressing a skinned clove of garlic through a garlic press. The crushed clove can be scraped off the press straight into a casserole or sauce and mixed with the other ingredients.

Using the tip of a knife to crush half or a whole clove of skinned garlic with a sprinkling of salt. Place all the pressure of the finger tip towards the tip of the knife.

Crushing biscuits into crumbs with a rolling pin. Place biscuits in a polythene bag to prevent crumbs flying around. Use the same method for crushing baked bread crusts.

Using a pestle and mortar to crush spices. This special strong bowl and crusher is often used to pound and blend spices for curry and other Eastern dishes.

Decorate

To make a dish look more attractive and appetising. Generally, 'decorating' applies to sweet dishes – pastries, cakes and desserts. Some decorations are traditional in form: with others you can use your imagination.

Using pastry trimmings to decorate a covered pie with a tassel. Cut a strip 2·5 cm (1 in) wide and 15 cm (6 in) long. Slash as shown, roll up and open out the fringe.

Making leaves from pastry trimmings. Roll out thinly 2·5 cm (1 in) wide strips and cut into diamond shapes. Mark the veins of the leaves with the back of a knife.

Adding the final touch of halved unskinned grapes to a Swiss roll that has been piped with rosettes of whipped cream. Place grapes, pips removed, cut side uppermost.

Piping melted chocolate in squiggles over alternate meringue shells on top of a vacherin (meringue cake).

➡

Making chocolate caraque. Melt the chocolate, pour on to a marble slab or melamine-type chopping board, and spread thinly. When almost set, shave off scrolls with a long sharp knife, held at a slight angle and away from yourself.

Using the chisel edge on a grater to make chocolate curls from the flat side of the block, for decorating the top of a sweet mousse. Pipe a border of whipped cream.

Marking the veins on a chocolate leaf. Melt the chocolate, pour into a baking tray lined with non-stick paper and spread thinly. When firm use the cutter, dipped in warm water and wiped dry.

Decorating a cold sweet lemon soufflé with bunches of frosted redcurrants (See FROST).

Topping a Dundee type cake mixture with blanched almonds (see BLANCH) and walnut halves before baking.

Setting glacé cherries, diamond shapes of angelica and toasted almonds into glacé icing that has been poured over a cooled but still warm Swedish yeast ring.

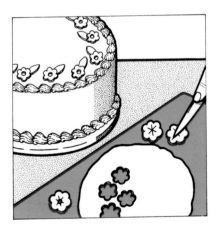

Marking the petals of almond paste flowers with the point of a knife. Cut out the shapes with a small fluted cutter, having tinted the almond paste, if wished, with food colouring before rolling out.

Using the 'wrong' end of a metal piping nozzle to cut holly leaves from green tinted almond paste. Mark down the centres with a knife and add berries rolled from red tinted paste.

Dice
To cut into small, cube-shaped pieces as even in size as possible.

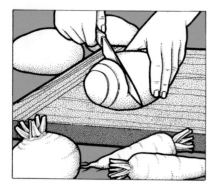

Cutting a potato into slices of even thickness. When the slicing is complete, cut each slice lengthways and crossways to produce dice.

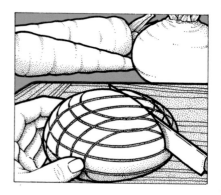

Holding a cut onion securely together and making the final series of crossways cuts to produce dice.

Dissolve
To mix a dry or solid ingredient with a liquid, applying heat if required, until a clear solution is obtained.

1

Sprinkling measured gelatine powder on to a specified amount of water in a small bowl.

2

Applying indirect heat by sitting the small bowl in a basin or pan (off the heat) of hot water in order to melt the gelatine. Dissolved gelatine must be the same temperature as the mixture it is added to.

Drain

Drain To remove any surplus liquid or fat from foods by using a sieve, colander, draining spoon or spatula, or by placing foodstuffs on kitchen paper towel.

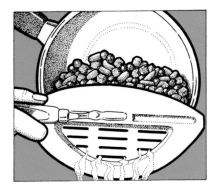

Draining the cooking water off vegetables through a special pan strainer. Alternatively use a colander or strong sieve, or even the lid if carefully used.

Using a slotted spoon to transfer freshly cooked fruit fritters from the hot fat on to kitchen paper towel which will absorb the excess fat.

Draw

Draw To prepare a plucked and hung bird for cooking. Usually the feet are removed, the sinews in the legs drawn, the head and neck cut off, and the gullet and windpipe loosened before removing the internal organs.

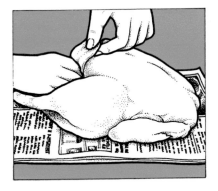

Pulling out the entrails through the enlarged tail end vent of the bird. Wipe out the body and keep the gizzard, heart and liver (with yellow gall bladder removed) for stock.

Dredge

Dredge To sprinkle food lightly and evenly with flour or sugar. Fish and meat are often dredged with flour before frying, and cakes and desserts with sugar to improve their appearance.

Using a finely perforated metal dredger to sprinkle icing sugar over a chocolate iced cake. Use strips of greaseproof paper to obtain a striped finish. These strips are carefully removed after dredging.

Dress

To garnish food attractively for serving; to add an oil based dressing to salads; to season and rearrange cooked shell fish meat in their shells. The term also means to pluck, draw and truss poultry and game.

1

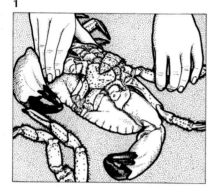

Laying a crab on its back and holding it firmly by the shell while removing the claws.

2

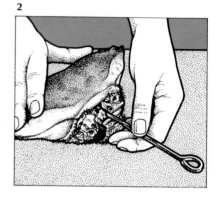

Loosening the body from the shell with a skewer before removing it and discarding the grey-white fronds (see step 3). Crack the claws and reserve the white flesh.

3

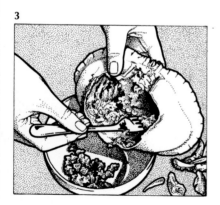

Scraping the dark meat carefully from the shell, after first removing the stomach bag which lies just below the head.

4

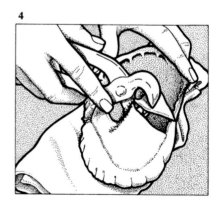

Chipping away the edge of the shell with pincers as far as the natural line. Season the light and dark meat separately and replace it in the shell.

Fillet

To remove the flesh of fish from the backbone, the breast of meat from poultry or the undercut of a loin of beef, pork, etc. The resulting boneless pieces of flesh are known as fillets.

1

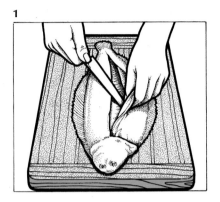

Taking the first of four fillets from a flat fish. Make a cut down the backbone through the flesh then separate the flesh with long sharp strokes to the bone. Cut below the head and above the tail to free the fillet.

2

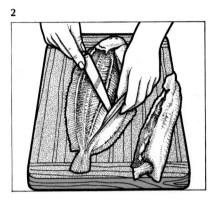

Having turned the fish round, this time work from the tail towards the head to remove the second fillet. Turn the fish over and remove the other two fillets in the same way.

1

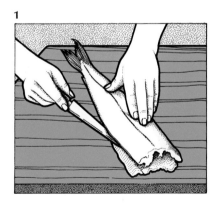

Cutting down to the bone along the centre back of a cleaned round fish. Use the knife to slice the top side of the flesh cleanly from the bones. Cut off the fillet at the tail.

2

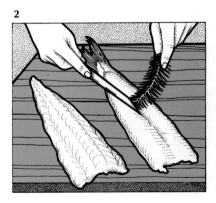

Using the knife to help ease off the backbone to give the second fillet. Cut off the tail.

Fillet *continued*

1

Removing the first fillet of breast meat from a chicken. Cut along one side of the breast bone and then work cleanly down close to the carcass to loosen the fillet in one piece.

2

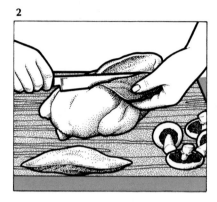

Cutting the second fillet from the other side of the breast in a similar way, having reversed the bird.

Flake To separate cooked fish into small pieces or to cut hard foodstuffs into thin slivers.

Holding a cooked fillet of fish steady with one fork and using another to pull away bits of flesh – it will break into natural divisions.

Cutting almonds that have been softened in a bowl of hot water into wafer like slices, after draining well. Almonds can also be bought ready flaked.

Flambé

To ignite and burn brandy, a liqueur or sherry poured over cooked food, like Christmas pudding, or into a pan with food being cooked to give flavour. As the alcohol burns the food absorbs the flavour of the alcohol.

Lighting brandy in a warmed metal spoon or ladle before pouring it over a pan of sautéed veal, small onions and mushrooms. This removes excess fat too.

Tilting a pan of crêpes Suzette, cooked in orange butter sauce, in order to ignite the liqueur, usually Grand Marnier.

Fold in

To combine a whisked or whipped mixture with other ingredients so that it retains its lightness. Do not agitate the mixture more than necessary or the air bubbles will break down and it will become flat.

Piling all the whisked egg whites on top of a soufflé mixture. Then, using a metal spoon, cut down through the mixture across the bottom and lift some mixture up over the egg white.

Sieving flour over whisked egg and sugar for a fatless sponge, and folding it in with a metal spoon. Folding in cannot be done with an electric mixer.

Freeze

To preserve suitable fresh foodstuffs and cooked dishes for a length of time by chilling and storing at 0°F (−18°C) or below. Various foods need treating and packing in different ways before freezing.

Placing hulled fresh strawberries on a baking sheet. Open freeze (i.e. uncovered) until hard then transfer into polythene freezer bags. Seal, label and return to the freezer.

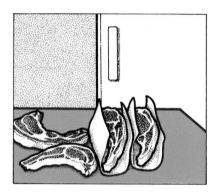

Interleaving chops with sheets of waxed paper, freezer film or foil before packing in a polythene bag or rigid container, so that they can be separated more easily when required.

Packing individual polythene lunch boxes into a chest type freezer. Save time and effort by making a week's supply of sandwiches, cake and drinks, etc. at one go and storing them in the freezer.

Extracting the air from a cake-filled polythene freezer bag with a freezer pump. Alternatively, the air can be sucked out through a drinking straw.

Frost

To give a crisp sparkling coat to fruits such as grapes or redcurrants, or to frost the rims of drinking glasses by dipping them first in egg white and then in sugar. Frosting is also an American cake icing.

Decorating the rim of a drinking glass by dipping it first in a bowl of very lightly whisked egg white and then in a bowl of caster or granulated sugar. Leave to dry before using.

Coating a small bunch of grapes in very lightly whisked egg white before dusting with caster sugar. Leave to dry before using as a decoration or for dessert. Use on the day of making.

Spreading the top and sides of a cake with American frosting. Use a knife to make soft swirls. This type of icing dries with a crisp outside but remains soft and marshmallowlike inside.

Froth

To sprinkle or dredge flour over a roasting joint or bird before heating and basting it in a hot oven, giving an even brown colour. Also to activate dried yeast.

Sprinkling a measured amount of dried yeast granules on to a measured quantity of warm sugar and water solution. Leave the mixture in a warm place until it froths well.

Fry
To cook food in hot fat or oil, either by immersing it completely as in deep fat frying, or by using less fat in a shallow pan and turning the food over to fry on both sides.

Deep frying fritters in oil or lard, using a thermometer to check the temperature. Cook at the correct temperature, about 190°C (375°F), to avoid soggy results.

Lifting partly fried potato chips out of the hot deep fat. Use a wire basket so that the chips can be lowered into the pan, raised and drained easily; ready for the second fry to achieve perfect results.

Pouring pancake batter into a pan, with just enough hot lard or oil to grease the base so that the batter will not stick.

Carefully placing fish cakes in heated shallow fat. Use sufficient fat to come halfway up the sides of the food.

Garnish

To improve the appearance and sometimes flavour of a dish by adding a complimentary edible garnish. This may be as simple as chopped parsley or watercress or as elaborate as 'turned' mushrooms.

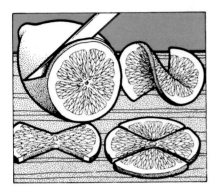

Slicing a lemon to make twists and butterflies. For a twist, cut to the centre of a slice from one side and twist the halves in opposite directions. For butterflies, cut out two triangular pieces from each slice.

Cutting radish roses by making about six cuts through each radish to its base. Leave in ice cold water to open up. Cut petal snips for radish waterlilies. Make the concertina shape by cutting along the length almost through and leave in iced water.

Twisting a cucumber slice into a cone after making one cut to the centre. Make a deckled edge by scoring the skin with a fork before slicing (See CRIMP).

Cutting gherkins to make fans. Drain the gherkins first and then slice each gherkin three or four times lengthways, almost to the stalk end. Gently fan out the slices.

Making zig-zag cuts in a firm tomato. Pull carefully in half and use tomato waterlilies to garnish a salad. Try cutting tomatoes as shown right and inserting slices of hard-boiled egg (See SLICE).

Cutting 5-cm (2-in) lengths of celery in narrow strips almost to the end to make tassels. For spring onions, include some green and trim the root first. Leave the cut vegetables in cold water to encourage curling.

Using a potato peeler to cut wafer thin strips of carrot to make curls to garnish sandwiches. Curl the strips, secure with a cocktail stick and leave in iced water to set the curls.

'Turning' button mushrooms to garnish grilled meat. Trim the stalk level with the cap. Make curved cuts from the top to the base of the cap, following the shape of the cap. Sauté in butter.

Shaping butter pats for garnishing grilled meats or fish. Use wooden 'hands' to make balls; a scalloped cutter for rounds; a special curler for cylinders. Chill until needed.

Garnishing pizzas with cheese, slivers of anchovy (See SLIVER), and black olives or tomato slices before baking. Use quick-melting cheese – Gruyère, Bel Paese or (best) Mozzarella.

Dicing slices of bread, after removing the crusts, to make fried croûtons. Make the dice about 0·5–1 cm (¼–½ in) square. Deep fry (See FRY) and use to garnish soup.

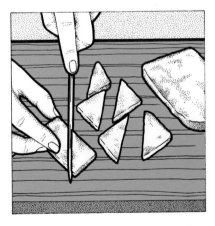

Cutting slices of fried bread into small triangles to garnish minced meat dishes, fricassees or stews. Remove the crusts before frying the bread.

Glaze

To give a glossy surface to sweet or savoury dishes either before or after cooking. Various substances are used for different foods.

Giving an attractive shiny coating of sugar syrup to hot cross buns immediately after they have been taken from the oven.

Glazing scones prior to baking with beaten egg. Milk can also be used.

Spooning clear arrowroot glaze over a prepared fruit flan. This type of syrup must be thick enough to cover so that it does not soak into the pastry. Use while still warm as it sets quickly.

Brushing warmed and sieved apricot jam over the top and sides of a cooked fruit cake before covering the cake with almond paste.

Grate

To shave food into small shreds using a special grater. The food should be hard or firm for easy grating. The size of the shred is controlled by the size of the holes or cutters on the grater.

Grating parboiled potatoes on a coarse grater for making Swiss rosti which consists of grated potato, seasoned and fried to a flat round shape in a frying pan. (See PARBOIL.)

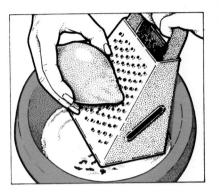

Grating the rind of a lemon straight into a soufflé mixture, using a fine cutter. Grate the outer rind only – not the pith.

Using a very fine cutter to grate nutmeg evenly over a custard tart. Freshly grated whole nutmeg cannot be bettered.

Using the coarse cutter on a grater to make small curls of chocolate from a slab for decoration.

➡️

Grate continued

Turning the handle of a small rotary hand grater to shred small pieces of cheese. This method is quick and easy and avoids damaging finger tips.

Grill To cook food under direct heat or over a hot fire. The grill should be well heated before use and then adjusted as required while the food is being cooked.

Arranging trimmed chops and tomatoes on the grid of a grill pan with cooking tongs. Season and brush the food with oil or melted fat before grilling and snip the fat on the meat to assist cooking.

Grind To reduce hard dry food-stuffs such as nuts, coffee beans, spices etc. to small particles by using a foodmill, a pestle and mortar or an electric grinder.

Using the end of a rolling pin to grind whole peppercorns against the base and sides of a heavy basin as an alternative to a special pestle and mortar (See POUND).

Measuring freshly ground coffee beans from an electric grinder into the filter of a coffee maker. Use this type of machine for grinding shelled nuts and whole spices, kept specially for the purpose.

Gut To remove the entrails from fish and to clean out the fish before cooking.

1

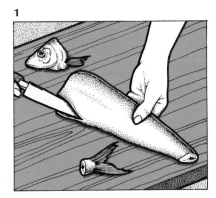

Using a sharp kitchen knife to slit open the soft belly of a fish down two thirds of its length, having first cut off the head and tail.

2

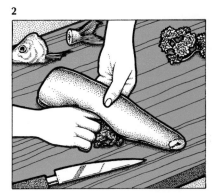

Holding the fish firmly in one hand to remove the entrails by running finger and thumb along the slit. Open out the fish and clean it under running cold water.

Hang To suspend meat or game in a cool, dry, airy place to make it more tender and flavoursome. Meat is usually sold ready hung; game may or may not be, so ask your poulterer. Game birds are hung by the neck; hares by the feet.

Hanging game birds until tender, when the tail or breast feathers will pull out easily. Hanging time varies with the bird, its age, the weather and personal taste – from a day to two weeks.

Hull To remove the calyx and stem from soft fruit such as strawberries.

Removing the calyx gently from ripe strawberries. Hull the fruit while it is firm and fresh, and handle it as little as possible.

Ice

To cover cakes and biscuits, usually with an icing sugar mixture, to enhance appearance and flavour. Icing used includes royal, glacé and butter cream.

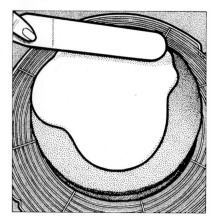

Spreading glacé icing all over a cake with a palette knife. Stand it on a wire rack. Let icing flow over the cake, then ease down the sides. Scrape up the surplus and use again if no crumbs are visible.

Pouring glacé icing from a wooden spoon to cover just the top of a cake. A greaseproof paper collar prevents the icing running down the sides and gives a thicker layer.

1

Spreading soft butter cream over a sandwich cake with a spatula or palette knife. Spread the butter cream over the sides of the cake too, if wished.

2

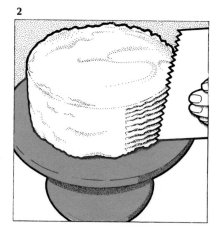

Decorating the sides by drawing a serrated plastic icing comb slightly up and down round the cake. Place the cake on a turntable to make this easier.

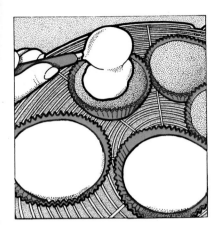

Pouring glacé icing on to little cakes cooked in paper cases. It should find its own level and leave a smooth finish. (For best results, make sure the tops of the cakes are flat.)

Dipping cream-filled éclairs across melted chocolate icing. Allow the surplus chocolate to run off and leave the éclairs to dry on a wire rack.

1

Levelling royal icing on top of a cake with a metal or plastic ruler. Draw it evenly and steadily across the cake at an angle of 45°. Trim off surplus icing. Leave to dry for about 24 hours before icing the sides.

2

Spreading royal icing on the sides of the cake, using a plain or serrated icing comb at an angle of about 45°. Rotate the turntable in the opposite direction to the hand holding the comb.

Infuse

To extract flavour from flavouring vegetables, herbs, spices, tea or coffee etc. by pouring on them a boiling or near boiling liquid and then leaving to stand in a warm place until the liquid is flavoured.

Bringing milk up to the boil with chopped vegetables, peppercorns and bay leaves. Remove from the heat and leave to infuse before straining and making béchamel sauce.

Leaving spices to stand after pouring boiling sugar syrup, wine or fruit juice over them so that they flavour the liquid for making a hot or cold punch.

Joint

To divide poultry, game birds or small animals such as hares and rabbits into suitable portions for cooking.

1

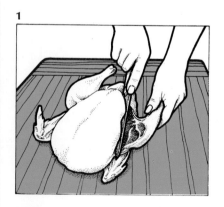

2

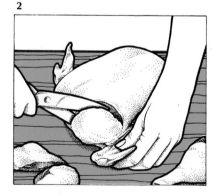

Removing the legs is the first step in jointing a turkey. Use a sharp knife to cut through the skin between leg and breast. Bend the leg outwards to break joint then cut free.

Using poultry shears to remove a wing together with a good portion of the breast meat. Cut down from the breast towards the wing joint.

3

Cutting through the natural break in the carcass to remove the whole of the remaining breast section. The lower part of the carcass can be used to make stock, after first cutting away the little cushions of flesh either side of the carcass.

4

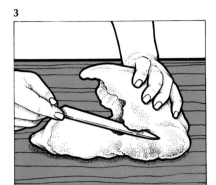

Turning the breast upside down and cutting down through the breast bone to divide it into two equal parts. Use a weight to knock the knife through the bone initially.

Knead

Knead To combine a mixture of ingredients which is too stiff to stir. Kneading distributes the yeast evenly in a bread dough and strengthens it for a good rise. Pastry and scone doughs should be handled lightly.

1

Collecting the mixture together ready to knead the pastry or scone dough on a lightly floured board. Flour the hands too to prevent the dough from sticking.

2

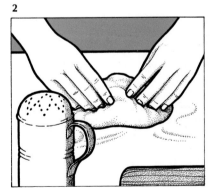

Kneading the dough lightly with the finger tips, turning it as you knead. Continue until the ingredients are mixed evenly – always be light handed with the dough. Remember to take the outer edges into the middle when kneading. ➡

1

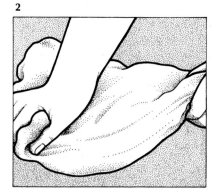

Kneading a bread dough. This benefits from firm handling. Flour the working surface, pull the dough out with one hand and fold it back on to itself.

2

Pulling and stretching out the dough, kneading firmly with the heel of the hand. Fold again, give a quarter turn and continue to knead until the dough feels elastic and smooth.

Knock up
To make horizontal cuts with the back of a knife blade in the sealed pastry edges of a covered or double-crust pie before baking.

Placing the first finger lightly on top of the pastry and using the other hand to tap sharply with the knife to give a raised, ridged edge to a pie.

Lard
To insert strips of fat bacon or pork into the flesh of meat or game to prevent it from becoming dry during cooking. Only lean meat or larger game birds need larding. Small game birds are better barded (See BARD).

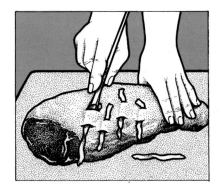

Threading narrow strips of fat with a special larding needle into a whole fillet of beef. Thread short lengths about 0·5 cm (¼ in) deep at intervals on all surfaces of the meat.

Lattice

To decorate the surface of a dish with a lattice pattern – particularly the top of an open tart or flan using rolled pastry trimmings. Use strips of anchovy on a pizza; piped cream on a trifle.

Laying a second layer of pastry strips at an angle to the first to create a simple criss-cross pattern. Moisten the ends and press them down well on to the pastry rim of the tart.

Creating an interwoven lattice. Fold back alternate strips of the first layer and add a strip at right angles. Replace folded-back strips, lift next ones and continue until complete.

Line

To give a protective or decorative covering to the base and sides of a cooking container – eg. with greaseproof or non-stick paper when baking cakes; with pastry when making flans; or with bacon for pâtés.

1

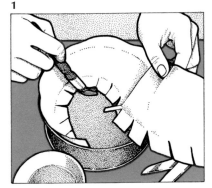

2

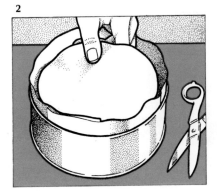

Lining the side of a greased, deep round cake tin with greaseproof paper. Cut the strip deeper than the tin. Fold a 2·5-cm (1-in) strip and make shallow cuts along it so that it fits round the base easily.

Placing a circle of greaseproof paper, cut to size, into the base of the tin. If the mixture is not rich, brush the paper with melted fat or oil before filling with cake mixture. ➡

Line *continued*

1

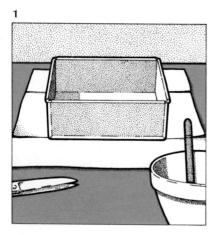

Placing a square tin in the centre of grease-proof paper, cut to the size of the base plus the depth of the sides. Cut from the sides in to each corner of the tin.

2

Fitting the paper which has been greased on the top side neatly into the greased tin, by overlapping the cut corners.

Use this method to line a Swiss roll tin.

1

Drawing round the base of a sandwich cake tin placed on a sheet of greaseproof paper. Cut out the greaseproof circle with a pair of kitchen scissors. Grease the base of the tin.

2

Placing the greaseproof circle in the baking tin and brushing the paper and side of the tin with oil. If preferred, the side of the tin may also be lined with a narrow strip of greaseproof.

Line continued

1

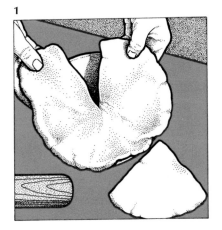

Lining a pudding basin with three-quarters of the prepared suet pastry; having cut out about a quarter after rolling out larger than the top of the basin. Ease the pastry into the basin overlapping the join and press to seal well.

2

Covering the filled pudding with the reserved pastry, having kneaded and rolled it out into a circle to fit. Turn in the top edge and dampen any overlapping pastry from the sides. Press edges together to seal.

1

Stretching rashers of rinded streaky bacon using a round bladed knife. Line the terrine with the bacon, leaving the ends overhanging the dish. Spoon in the pâté mixture.

2

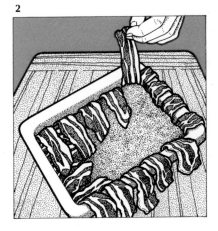

Folding the ends of the rashers over the filled dish before covering with the dish lid or foil and cooking.

Macerate

To soften foods by soaking them in a hot or cold liquid so that they swell up. Dried foods like lentils and other pulses and dried fruits are treated in this way before cooking. Using a boiling liquid speeds the process.

Pouring boiling water over dried apples, apricots and prunes to soften and plump them up, therefore reducing the cooking time a little.

Marinate

To steep raw meat, game or fish in a blend of oil, wine or vinegar, seasonings and vegetables (sometimes previously heated and cooled) for periods of an hour up to several days to make it more tender and flavoursome, and to give moisture to dry meats.

Pouring a wine marinade over raw chicken portions that have been placed in a polythene bag inside a deep bowl for support. Secure the bag with a twist tie and leave to marinate, turning the chicken occasionally.

Mask

To cover cold meat or fish with a savoury jelly, glaze or sauce to give an appetising appearance; to coat the inside of a mould with jelly; to protect part of a cake with paper before decorating the unmasked section.

1

Pouring a small quantity of cold liquid jelly into a mould placed in a bowl of ice cubes to accelerate setting.

2

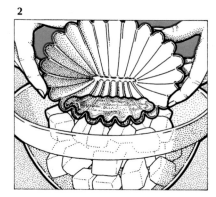

Tipping the mould carefully when the jelly begins to set so that it covers or masks the inside. Pour in more liquid jelly and repeat until all of the inside is coated.

Measure
To find the required amount of a recipe ingredient by using a calibrated jug for liquids, special kitchen measuring spoons for small amounts of solids and liquids, or scales for weighing larger quantities.

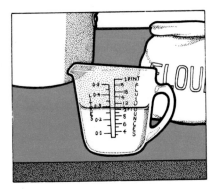

Using a jug marked in both fluid ounces and litres for measuring a liquid. A glass jug is easier to use. Always check the amount at eye level.

Pressing baking powder lightly into a spoon specially marked with its capacity in millilitres; levelling the powder off with a knife to obtain the exact amount.

Melt
To apply heat to a solid ingredient until it becomes softened or is liquified. It is often necessary to use the double boiler method.

1

2

Melting pieces of cooking chocolate in a bowl placed over a pan of hot water. Allow them to melt slowly. Do not overheat or the chocolate will lose its glossiness.

Preparing to pour the melted chocolate, before it starts to cool and thicken, over a layered cake. Brush the cake with apricot glaze first (See GLAZE).

Melt *continued*

Pouring melted butter over individual pâtés in order to seal them. Melt the butter over a low heat, taking care not to let it bubble or brown.

Mince To cut up food, using a mincing machine. Different sizes of discs (cutters) produce either coarse or finely minced results. To help clean the mincer, pass a piece of bread through at the end.

Passing cubes of meat through a hand-operated mincer which is held in place on the working surface by a suction pad. The fingers guide the food only at the start of each mincing.

Using a special wooden plunger to press the chopped vegetables, meat and parsley down into the hopper of an electric mincer whilst the mincer is operating.

Mix To combine two or more ingredients. Mixing can be performed by hand or with the aid of a spoon, knife, fork or a hand-held or stand-mounted electric food mixer.

Using a palette knife to mix a pastry dough, having sprinkled the required amount of cold water over the rubbed in fat and flour.

Parboil
To boil food (usually vegetables) for a short time before completing the cooking by some other method such as frying, roasting or braising.

Placing parboiled potatoes round a roast joint to finish cooking in the hot fat. Boil the potatoes for 5 minutes, drain well and then put them in the roasting tin to cook for about 1 hour.

Pare
To peel fruit or vegetables thinly or to trim them by cutting away any irregular parts.

Using a potato peeler to pare just the coloured part of the rind from an orange so that all the bitter-tasting white pith is left behind.

Peel
To remove the outer shell or rind from a variety of foods.

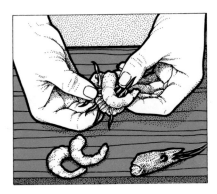

Taking a cooked prawn out of its shell. Gently break off the head and pull away the tail, then peel off the soft body shell by working round from the small claws on the underside.

Peeling an orange. Cut through the rind to the flesh so that it is marked into quarters. Pull back each section of rind, removing as much white pith as possible.

Pip To remove the pips or seeds from fruit before cooking or eating.

Using a small pointed knife to remove the pips from grapes, after first cutting them in half.

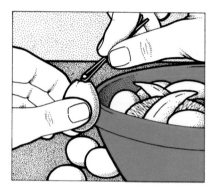

Taking pips out of whole grapes with a sterilized hair grip. Hold the grape firmly, insert the curved end of the grip at the stem end and draw it out gently with the pip.

Pipe To force a soft mixture through a bag and piping nozzle in order to shape it. The mixture must be of a consistency that holds its shape – whether icing for cakes, biscuit dough, creamed potato or choux paste.

1

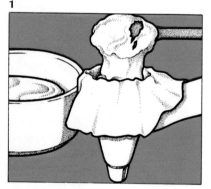

Spooning uncooked choux paste into a cloth or nylon piping bag fitted with a plain nozzle for making eclairs and choux buns. The cuff of the icing bag turns back over the hand for easy filling.

2

Pressing the filled bag firmly to extrude the mixture on to a greased baking sheet. When enough mixture is forced through the nozzle, cut it with a knife.

Piping duchesse potato mixture through a vegetable star nozzle. Press steadily and then lift the nozzle sharply off the mixture. (The hand under the bag is only held lightly as a guide: the pressure comes from the hand at the top.)

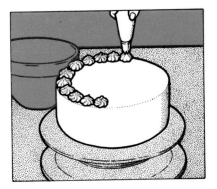

Using a small star nozzle to pipe rosettes on to an iced cake. Hold the upright nozzle close to the cake, press out a little icing and lift it up sharply with a slight twist.

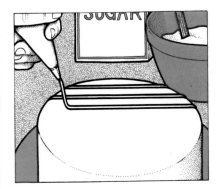

Piping straight lines of icing with a writing nozzle across the top of a cake. Hold the nozzle above the cake and guide the piped trail of icing into the correct place.

Decorating the base of a cake with a shell design using a shell or star nozzle. Pipe the shell with a well formed head and then gradually release the pressure and pull away leaving a tail.

Pluck
To remove the feathers from poultry and game birds. Just two or three feathers should be extracted at a time by pulling sharply against the way they lie.

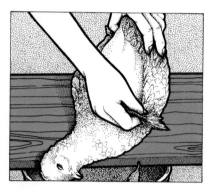

Beginning with the breast and working towards the head. Pluck the back next and, finally, the wings. Singe remaining hairs and tiny feathers with a lighted taper, then wipe with a damp cloth.

Poach
To cook gently in a liquid at a temperature of not more than 96°C (205°F) so that the surface is just trembling. It can be done in an open pan, in the oven or using the popular egg poacher with a lid.

Poaching apple rings in a prepared syrup. Add any extra sugar to sour fruits at the end of cooking time; poaching in too thick a syrup can toughen some fruit skins.

1

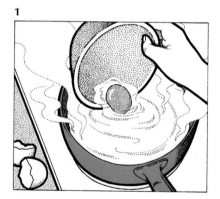

Sliding an egg into barely simmering water. Bring the water to the boil, lower the heat, stir rapidly and slide the egg into the centre of the swirl. A little salt and vinegar is sometimes added to the water.

2

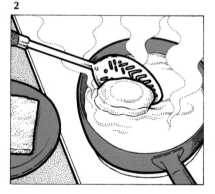

Lifting the neatly shaped poached egg from the water with a slotted spoon, having left it to cook for about 5 minutes or until the yoke has set and the white has become opaque.

Poach *continued*

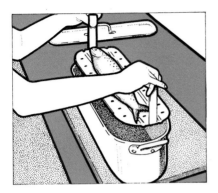

Lowering a fish on a rack into a fish kettle of boiling salted water or court bouillon. Reduce the heat and allow to simmer.

Pot roast

To cook meat in a covered pan or casserole with fat and a little liquid, on top of the cooker or in the oven. Pot roasting is good for small and less tender joints. The meat is first browned over a high heat.

Placing the evenly browned meat in a casserole. A flameproof casserole is best as the meat can be browned in it first. On the top of the cooker use a thick based pan. If liked, surround with prepared vegetables.

Pound

To crush or bruise in order to reduce a hard ingredient to small pieces or a soft one to a smooth consistency. Pounding can be done in a pestle and mortar or using a rolling pin (See GRIND).

Pounding kipper fillets with a pestle in a mortar to break them down to a suitable texture for a fish pâté.

Preform

To line a rigid container with a flexible wrapping material before filling with food for freezing. When frozen, the food is removed from the container, sealed and labelled, leaving the container free for further use.

1

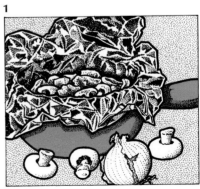

Filling a casserole lined with freezer foil with a cooked and cooled stew. The foil should be cut so that there is plenty of wrapover to enclose the stew.

➡

2

Taking the frozen stew out of the casserole and securing seams of wrap-over with freezer tape or over wrap, before labelling with description and date. To reheat, unwrap and replace in the same casserole.

1

Pouring fruit purée into a strong freezer bag placed in a polythene container, before freezing. Secure the top lightly with a coated twist tie, leaving space for expansion.

2

Removing the frozen fruit in its bag from the container. Check that the twist tie is holding firm and that all the air is excluded. Label and return the package to the freezer.

Preserve To treat fruit, vegetables and meat in order to keep them in a safe condition for a long period. Home preserving is usually done by heat application (jams, jellies, bottling), salting, drying or freezing.

Testing the set of jelly after a spoonful has been left to cool on a saucer. If the jelly wrinkles when a little finger is drawn through it, it is ready for pouring into pots for setting.

Preserve *continued*

Filling a jar with layers of sliced runner beans and salt to preserve the beans. Use a hopper to make filling the jar easy.

Threading peeled and cored apples on thin sticks for drying, after the slices have been soaked for 5 minutes in salted water. Dry in a cool oven for 6–8 hours or until leathery.

Press
To shape meat by pressing it under a weight. The cold pressed meat – often spiced beef or tongue, boned stuffed chicken or meat roll – is turned out and sometimes glazed. Some fruit desserts, eg. summer pudding, are also pressed.

Placing a saucer, smaller than the dish, with weights on top of a cooked tongue coiled into a dish. This presses it into a firm shape for turning out and glazing.

Using a special meat press clamped over a metal bowl to hold spiced beef firmly together as it cools. Pressed like this, the meat is easy to cut and has a close texture.

Prove

To allow a yeast dough to rise a second time. After the initial kneading, the dough is left to rise, 'knocked down', shaped for bread or rolls and left to rise again. This proving ensures an even textured loaf. (See also RISE.)

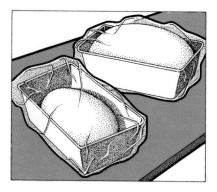

Proving loaves prior to baking. Shape dough to fit the greased loaf tins. Place inside an oiled polythene bag and leave until the dough has doubled in size – about 1 hour.

Covering unbaked shaped rolls with a lightly oiled polythene bag before leaving them to prove. The bag must be large enough to allow the dough to rise until it has doubled its size.

Pulp

To reduce food, usually fruit, to a soft consistency by gently cooking in very little liquid.

Using a potato masher to break down apple that has been cooked until soft. The masher roughly and speedily breaks down the food, but not as smoothly as sieving (See SIEVE).

Purée

To sieve, blend or pound raw or cooked foods so that they are of a creamy, lump-free texture. If using a sieve, a wire one may be used for meat and vegetables but a nylon one is best for fruit and tomatoes.

Pressing cooked vegetables through a coarse wire sieve with a wooden spoon in preparation for vegetable soup. Alternatively, purée the vegetables in an electric blender (liquidiser).

Purée *continued*

Puréeing fresh ripe raw or cooked apricots in a hand-operated food mill. It is easier to use a food mill when fruit has stones as these will be left behind.

Reduce
To fast boil a liquid in an uncovered pan to evaporate the surplus liquid and give a concentrated, richly flavoured result. Reducing is usually done when making sauces, soups and syrups.

Pouring reduced pan juices over sautéed meat and vegetables to glaze them. After cooking the meat and vegetables remove to a serving dish and keep warm. Reduce the juices in the cooking pan.

Refresh
To pour cold water over blanched and drained vegetables in order to set the colour and to stop the cooking process. Also to revive or keep salad ingredients, especially lettuce, crisp.

Running cold water from the tap over blanched and drained green beans.

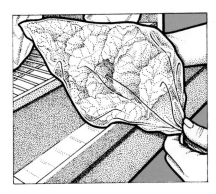

Refreshing lettuce in the refrigerator. Wash the leaves, shake off excess moisture, put in a polythene bag and place in the bottom of the refrigerator, preferably in the crisper drawer, for about an hour.

Render

To extract fat or clean dripping from fatty meat trimmings, by heating them in the oven or by boiling them in an uncovered pan with a little water until the water has evaporated and the fat is released.

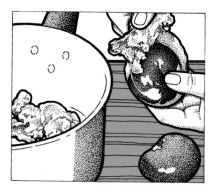

Pricking and pressing fatty trimmings that have been left to melt in a low oven, to help release the fat. Repeat this at regular intervals. Return to the oven until the fat runs freely then strain.

Peeling the fatty tissues from a kidney before putting the fat in a heavy pan with a little water. Boil until the water is driven off, leaving the melted fat. Strain into a clean bowl.

Rise

To allow a yeast dough to double in size before baking. When it has risen, the dough is sometimes knocked down, shaped and then allowed to rise for a second time – also known as proving (See PROVE).

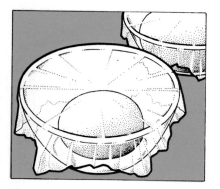

Leaving the kneaded dough to rise in a bowl covered with cling film or oiled polythene. The time required ranges from under an hour in a warm place to 24 hours in a refrigerator.

Roast

To cook food – usually meat, poultry or game – by radiant heat in an oven or on a spit. Cooking time is calculated from the weight of the joint which can be quick or slow roasted (See also SPIT ROAST and page 7).

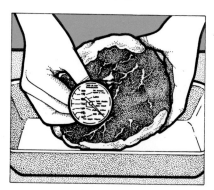

Placing a meat thermometer into the centre of a joint, avoiding the bone. When the dial pointer shows the correct temperature, the meat is done.

Roast *continued*

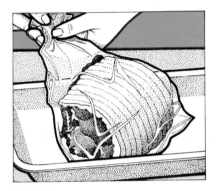

Using a transparent roasting bag to eliminate splashing in the oven. The meat browns through the bag. Sprinkle the inside with flour before fastening and nicking the top of the bag.

Roll out To flatten pastry, dough, etc to the required thickness, shape and size using a rolling pin or similar cylindrical utensil. Use short, light strokes and, if time permits, chill rich mixtures in the refrigerator first.

Rolling out shortcrust pastry to size on a lightly floured surface. Use an even pressure and make short firm rolls in one direction only. Dust the rolling pin with flour – never the pastry.

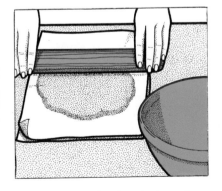

Preventing a rich shortbread mixture from sticking by rolling it out between two sheets of greaseproof, waxed or non-stick paper. Turn the mixture after each rolling to ensure a perfect round.

Roll up To roll a cooked or raw mixture on to itself making a cylinder shape. The mixture may be first spread with a filling or stuffing or may be left to be filled later.

Rolling a brandy snap over the greased handle of a wooden spoon while the mixture is still warm but not crisp. When cold, fill the hollow with whipped cream. ➡

Roll up _continued_

1

Preparing the baked sponge for a Swiss roll. Turn out immediately after baking on to a sheet of greaseproof paper sprinkled with caster sugar and trim off the crusty edges. Spread with warm jam.

2

Rolling up the sponge, having half cut through it about 1 cm (½ in) from one of the short ends. This ensures the sponge rolls tightly. Roll quickly, pushing on the paper.

Rub in To incorporate fat into
flour when making shortcrust pastry, plain cakes or biscuits, when a short texture is required. A rubbed in mixture should look and feel like fine breadcrumbs.

Rubbing fat into flour. First cut the fat into smallish pieces, season and sieve the flour if necessary, then rub in the fat lightly with the tips of the fingers.

Salt To sprinkle with salt either for
seasoning or, as in the case of aubergines, to draw out excess moisture and to remove any bitter-tasting juices. To salt is also a classic method of preserving meat and fish.

Sprinkling slices of aubergine with salt. Score the cut surface first to allow the salt to penetrate. Leave for at least 30 minutes before rinsing and drying.

Sauté

To fry lightly in a little butter and/or oil, sometimes adding a little stock towards the end of cooking. A sauté pan has a wide base which allows plenty of room. Alternatively, use a frying pan with a lid.

Using a pair of cooking tongs to turn chicken joints over in hot fat while preparing them for a casserole dish.

Scald

To pour boiling water over fruit (eg. tomatoes, peaches) to make it easy to remove skins, and over pork to loosen the hairs from its skin or to treat trotters. Remove food before it cooks. Also to treat milk or to cleanse jelly bags.

Heating milk or cream in a double saucepan to a temperature just below boiling point to retard souring. Scalded cream forms a soft crust which is pleasant to eat, eg. clotted cream.

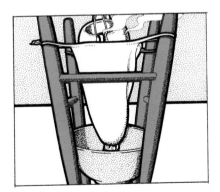

Pouring boiling water through a jelly bag to scald or cleanse it thoroughly, both before and after it is used for straining cooked fruit to make jelly.

Pouring water, three parts boiling and one part cold, on to pig's trotters in order to clean them and loosen hairs for easy removal.

Scallop

To decorate the double edge of the pastry covering of a pie. Traditionally the scallop for sweet dishes should be small and for savoury pies wider apart.

Using a small round-bladed or table knife to scallop pastry. First make horizontal cuts round the edge (See KNOCK UP), then pull the pastry edge vertically with the knife and at the same time use the thumb to make the scallop.

Score

To make shallow cuts in the surface of food, to help it cook more quickly, to improve appearance, to enable it to absorb flavours better or to aid cutting after baking.

Cutting the fat of a skinned, almost-cooked bacon joint in a diamond pattern. Pat with brown sugar or other glaze, stud with cloves (See STUD) and return to a hot oven for about 20 minutes.

Making a series of parallel cuts about 1 cm (½ in) apart in the rind of a loin of pork, to encourage crackling and to facilitate carving. Use a very sharp knife.

Marking the sections on an uncooked shortbread to make it easier to break after baking. Similarly, fudge and toffee are marked before completely set to aid cutting.

Scrape
To remove the top or outer layer of food – particularly of fruit and vegetables – in preparation for cooking.

Drawing the blade of a small vegetable knife down the stem of asparagus using quick, light movements. Avoid cutting into the asparagus.

Seal
To fry or sear meat in hot fat in order to add flavour and give colour to the outer edges before braising or casseroling; to encase a filling in pastry or other coating; to exclude air from jam in a pot by sealing the top with a waxed disc.

Pressing two edges of pastry firmly together over a filling. First moisten the edge of the lower round of pastry with water or milk so the two edges stick together and ensure a good seal.

Sear
To brown meat or poultry quickly in hot fat before casseroling, braising or stewing. This sealing of the meat gives the finished dish a better colour and flavour.

Browning pieces of seasoned or marinated (See MARINATE) meat in hot fat in a flameproof dish for a stew. Add the vegetables and liquid afterwards, and cook slowly in the oven or over a low heat.

Season
To add, usually, salt and pepper but sometimes other flavourings (herbs, spices, etc) to a dish in order to enhance its taste. Also to clean and condition a cast iron frying or omelette pan.

Cleaning a plain cast iron frying pan by heating it and rubbing in salt with kitchen paper towel, or warming a film of oil in the pan and rubbing with kitchen paper towel. ➡

Season *continued*

Adding freshly ground pepper straight from a pepper mill to a white sauce. Taste after each addition.

Seed To remove seeds from fruit or vegetables. It is usual to take the core away at the same time, especially if the vegetable is to be stuffed. Use either a sharp knife or a teaspoon, depending on the ripeness and texture.

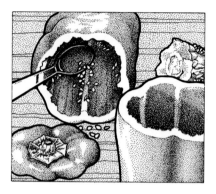

Removing the seeds from a green or red pepper with a small spoon, having first cut off the stalk end. The seeded pepper can be sliced or stuffed.

Segment To divide the flesh of citrus fruits into natural portions or segments, removing the skin and pith. In a fruit salad, the segments are easier to eat if they are cut away from the membrane and core.

1

Removing the peel from an orange. Place the orange on a board and, using a sharp knife, cut downwards from the stem end, removing with the peel as much pith as possible, to reveal the juice sacs.

2

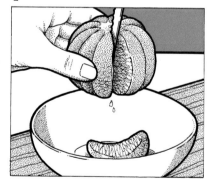

Separating each segment from its skin or membrane with a sharp knife. Cut towards the centre core, as close as possible to the membrane on each side of the segment, and let the segment and juice fall into a bowl.

Segment *continued*

1

Loosening the flesh of a halved grapefruit from the outer skin and pith with a curved, serrated grapefruit knife. Run the knife round, leaving the flesh free of pith. Remove the pips.

2

Loosening the segments from the membranes so they can be eaten with a teaspoon. Cut as near as possible to the membrane on both sides of each segment.

Separate
To divide or remove something from another. This term is used especially when dividing the yolk and white of an egg so that each can be used separately, as in soufflés and meringues.

1

Tapping an egg sharply on the side of a pudding basin prior to separating the yolk from the white. Use the thumb to prise the cracked not broken edge of the shell apart.

2

Breaking the egg shell carefully in two to retain the yolk in one half while the white falls into a bowl. Tip the yolk gently back and forth between the half shells until all the white is removed. ➡

Separate *continued*

Using a wine glass to separate an egg. Break the egg carefully on to a saucer, cover the yolk with an upturned wine glass. Tip the white into a bowl, lifting the edge of the glass slightly to free any remaining white.

Breaking an egg into a special egg separator placed over a cup. This gadget has a slit in it which allows the egg white to fall through, while retaining the yolk.

Shell To crack and remove the shell or hard outer skin of foods such as nuts and hard-boiled eggs.

Peeling off the shell of a hard-boiled egg after cracking it gently. Plunge the egg into cold water immediately it is cooked and the shell will come away more easily.

Cracking nuts with a special nut-cracker so that the shell can be removed. Use a nut-cracker with care so the kernel will remain whole and the shell will come away easily.

Shirr
To cook food, often eggs, in small shallow dishes or ramekins in the oven. Shirred eggs, sometimes called 'oeufs sur le plat', are popular in the USA.

Cooking eggs in greased ramekins placed in a fairly hot oven. Season, spooning over cream or melted butter and a few bread-crumbs, before baking. The eggs are ready to eat when lightly set.

Shred
To cut food finely with a sharp knife or on a coarse grater. Shredded food is in larger strips than grated food.

Cutting orange and grapefruit peel into shreds for marmalade, after the pith and flesh has been removed. Use a short sharp vegetable knife to do this.

Shredding quarters of a firm cabbage prior to cooking or for using raw in salads. Use a long sharp kitchen knife. (Slice with or across the grain depending on the length of shreds needed.)

Sieve
To purée cooked food by pressing it through a wire or nylon sieve. Use a wooden spoon to press the food through. Do not try sieving too much food at one time.

Pressing cooked potatoes through a fairly coarse wire sieve with a wooden spoon. This is the best way to prepare potatoes for Duchesse potatoes.

Sift

To shake a dry ingredient such as flour or sugar through a sieve or special sifter in order to remove any lumps and, in some cases, to incorporate air.

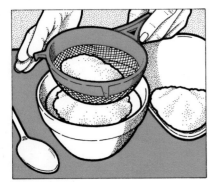

Sifting flour on to a mixture of whisked egg and sugar for a fatless sponge. Tip the measured flour into a sieve and tap the edge lightly with one hand.

Simmer

To keep liquid just below boiling point, about 96°C (205°F). To cook by way of simmering, the food is brought to the boil in a liquid and then the temperature is reduced to a simmer.

Simmering a pan of stock and rice for risotto. Note that the liquid just moves or murmurs with the occasional bubble – if it bubbles (lefthand pan) the temperature is too high and the liquid is boiling.

Skewer

To thread chunks of meat, poultry, offal, seafood and/or vegetables on to a skewer for grilling, as in kebabs, or to use metal or wooden (not plastic) skewers to hold joints of meat, poultry or fish in shape during cooking.

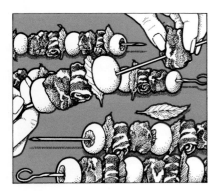

Impaling cubes of raw meat, bacon rolls, mushrooms and bay leaves for grilling. Flat or twisted skewers, previously greased, prevent the food slipping round when the kebabs are turned.

Using wooden cocktail sticks to secure the savoury stuffing in the belly of a fish prior to cooking.

Skim

To remove excess fat from gravy, soup or stew, and froth from stock, while cooking. To remove the scum from jam or to take the cream off milk.

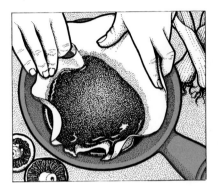

Removing the scum from a pan of hot jam by skimming lightly over the surface with a flattish perforated spoon. Spoon the scum on to a saucer held near the pan.

Blotting up the fat from a pan of stew using thick absorbent kitchen paper.

Skin

To strip or remove the outer coat or skin from a variety of foods such as fish, poultry, meat and fruits. When skinning fish, prevent fingers from slipping by dipping them in salt.

Lifting the skin off a piece of salmon, after it has been cooked and allowed to cool. Use a knife to separate the skin from the flesh at one corner and pull, easing away gently.

Drawing back the skin of a round fish towards the tail. First cut the skin and loosen it below the head with a knife. Sever the skin at the tail. Repeat on the other side. ➡

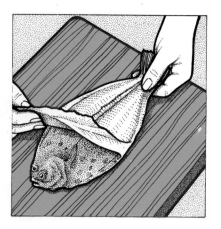

Pulling the dark skin of a sole quickly and firmly from the tail towards the head. First cut a slit below the tail and loosen the skin with the thumb.

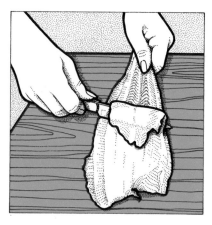

Skinning a fillet of fish. Hold firmly by the tail, skin side down. With a sharp knife, use a scraping movement along the skin, easing the flesh away from you.

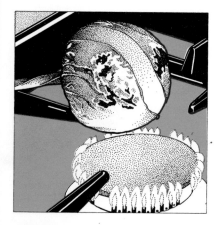

Holding a tomato on the prongs of a fork or a skewer over an open gas flame until it splits. Turn the tomato slowly all the time. Peel away the charred skin with the fingers.

Skinning tomatoes by plunging them into a basin of boiling water for a few seconds. Lift out with a spoon and peel away the softened skin with the fingers. When skinning many tomatoes, cool them with cold water to prevent cooking.

Pulling the skin away from the flesh of a chicken piece, having first loosened a corner of it with the tip of a knife to get a firm grip.

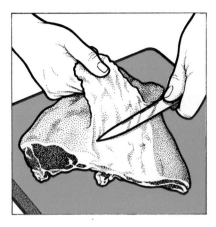

Using a sharp knife to remove the skin from a loin of lamb while pulling it free with the other hand.

Peeling away a grape skin from the stalk end with a small sharp knife. If difficult to remove, treat like tomatoes by plunging the grapes briefly into boiling water.

Slash To make shallow cuts with a knife in foods prior to cooking to help heat to penetrate, steam to escape and to add to the decorative appearance.

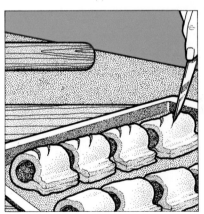

Using a sharp knife to make a couple of neat cuts in the top of sausage rolls before putting them in the oven.

Slice

To cut foods into thin rounds or slices using a sharp kitchen knife or a specially designed gadget (see slicing hard-boiled egg).

Cutting a tomato with a serrated knife. Lay the tomato on its side so that the first slice takes off the stalk end. Slicing this way helps prevent the seeds from falling out.

Slicing an onion into rings. First cut off a thin piece from one side so that the onion can be placed flat on the board to stop it rolling about.

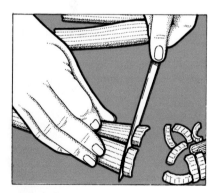

Holding stalks of celery in a bunch so that they can be sliced together more quickly. First cut thick stalk ends in two lengthways so the slices are all about the same size.

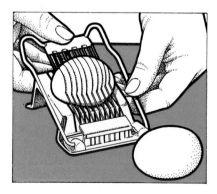

Using a special egg slicer to cut up a whole hard-boiled egg in one easy movement, producing perfect slices.

Sliver

To cut very fine strips of food, such as nuts or anchovy, for decoration or garnish, using a very sharp, medium sized kitchen knife.

Cutting halved almonds into slivers after skinning them and soaking them in hot water to make the nuts pliable. Almonds split naturally lengthways.

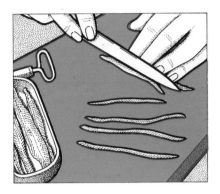

Using an extra sharp knife to cut very thin slices of anchovy fillet, carefully smoothing out the fillet first.

Snip

To cut foodstuffs into small pieces using a pair of kitchen scissors, or to cut into pastry etc with scissors at regular intervals to give a decorative effect, round the edge or over the top.

Cutting a bunch of rinsed fresh chives directly over a prepared potato salad to add both flavour and colour. A pair of kitchen scissors is the best implement to use.

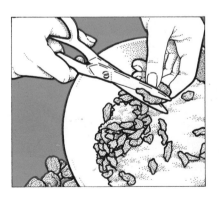

Using scissors, dipped in hot water, to cut up dried apricots to a suitable size for addition to stuffing.

➡

Snip *continued*

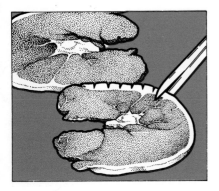

Cutting into the fat round the edge of a gammon rasher at 2·5-cm (1-in) intervals, to prevent it curling up during grilling or frying.

Souse

To pickle foods such as fish, pork or veal by cooking them in vinegar and spices and then allowing them to cool and stand in the same liquid.

Pouring a prepared marinade of vinegar and spices over rolled herring fillets in an ovenproof dish. Cover, bake, cool and then leave in the refrigerator for a few days.

Spit roast

To roast meat or poultry on a revolving spit over or under direct heat from an open fire, gas flame or electric element. Most electric spits are either combined with the grill unit or positioned in the oven.

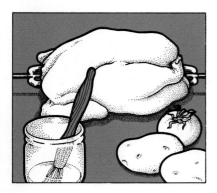

Preparing a chicken for spit roasting by impaling the bird *evenly* through the centre on a shaft fitted with holding forks. These are screwed tightly against the bird.

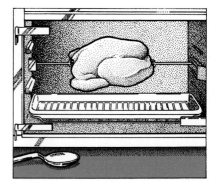

Putting the chicken on the shaft in position in an electric rôtisserie. During cooking, meat or poultry may be basted with juices from the drip tray, where potatoes can be baked at the same time.

Steam

To cook food in the steam from boiling water. This is a gentle and economical way of cooking and in the case of vegetables and fruit helps to conserve nutrients. Steaming is done in various ways.

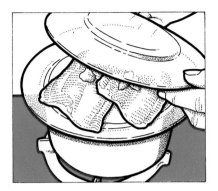

Steaming fillets of fish between two plates placed over a saucepan of boiling water. Add butter and seasoning before covering the fish.

Placing scrubbed, unpeeled new potatoes in a steamer with a perforated base designed to fit over a pan of boiling water. Cover with the saucepan lid.

Lowering a wire mesh basket into a pan of boiling water to steam cauliflower. The wire supports hold it in a raised position, clear of the water, while in use. This basket packs flat for storing.

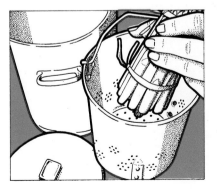

Using a tall steamer designed for cooking asparagus. Place the tied-up bundle of asparagus, tips uppermost, in the perforated basket. Lower it into the outer pan two-thirds filled with boiling water. Cover with the lid. ➤

1

Lowering a pudding into a saucepan for steaming, with hot water to come half way up the side of the basin. Stand the basin on an upturned saucer or crossed skewers to raise it from the bottom of the pan.

2

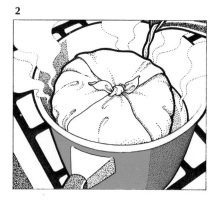

Topping up with boiling water, as the original water evaporates, during steaming. Make sure the water reaches half-way up the basin and keep the pan covered with its lid.

Placing custard cups in a shallow perforated steamer which can be used with an ordinary saucepan. The clip on one side of the handled steamer allows it to balance over the saucepan. Cover with the pan lid.

Stew
To cook meat, fish, vegetables or fruit very slowly in water or stock at simmering point. Meat stews, thickened or unthickened, can be brown (pre-fried meat) or white (meat placed straight into cold liquid).

Adding pieces of stewing lamb to vegetables and stock in a casserole. Cover with a tight fitting lid and simmer gently. Do not boil or the food will toughen or break up.

Stir
To mix gently with a circular movement – in most cases using a spoon.

Stirring chopped parsley into a white sauce with a wooden spoon.

Stone
To remove the stone from fruit such as cherries, peaches, apricots, avocados, etc. before cooking. Stones can be removed much more easily if the fruit is fully ripe.

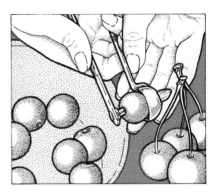

Pressing the stone out of a ripe cherry with a special cherry stoner. Remove the stalk, place the cherry in the cup end of the gadget and press sharply with the angled end.

Using a small pointed knife to lever the stone out of a ripe peach. First cut the fruit in half lengthways, i.e. from the stalk end. Gently twist the halves apart.

Strain
To clear a liquid of any solids by passing it through a sieve, colander or muslin cloth.

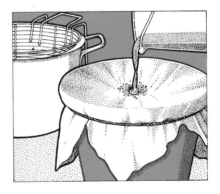

Pouring oil that has been used for deep frying through a muslin cloth, in order to remove any impurities, so that the oil may be used again.

➡

Strain *continued*

Straining an egg custard mixture through a wire sieve on to a prepared pastry case for a custard tart.

String
To remove the tough side pieces which connect the two halves of a runner bean pod, or to strip berries such as red, white or blackcurrants from their stalks.

Drawing the prongs of a fork down a spray of redcurrants to remove the berries easily and quickly from the stalk.

Stud
To stick cloves into vegetables, fruit or meat to impart flavour to the food and/or the liquid in which it is cooked. A dessert can be studded with decorations for eye appeal.

Pressing the stem of the cloves into a skinned onion for flavouring the milk for a bread sauce or béchamel sauce.

Sticking cloves into a parboiled gammon joint before baking it. Remove the skin and score the fat in a diamond pattern first. To look attractive, place a clove in alternate squares.

Stuff

To fill poultry, meat, fish or vegetables before cooking with a savoury mixture, usually based on breadcrumbs or rice, to impart flavour and give shape.

1

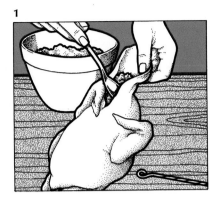

Spooning a stuffing into the cavity at the neck end of a chicken. Do not pack too tightly as the stuffing expands during cooking.

2

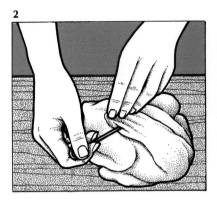

Folding over the flap of neck skin and securing it in place with a skewer. Alternatively, fold the tips of the wings over the flap to hold it in position.

1

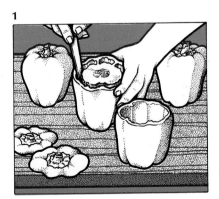

Cutting out the core and inner membranes from a sweet pepper with a sharp knife. First slice off the stalk end and reserve it for a 'lid'.

2

Filling the peppers with a rice-based savoury stuffing. Put on the reserved 'lid' and stand the peppers in an ovenproof dish with a little stock added. Brush with oil or melted fat and cover before cooking. ➡

1

2

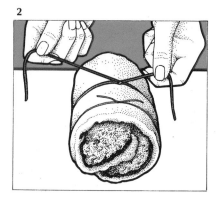

Using a knife to spread stuffing evenly over a breast of lamb. Leave the edges free of stuffing. Roll up from one end.

Tying lengths of thread, not too tightly, round the stuffed and rolled lamb to hold it together during cooking. Cut and remove the string before serving.

1

2

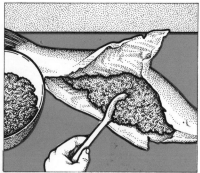

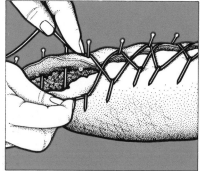

Stuffing the cavity left in the belly of a round fish after it has been gutted and cleaned.

Securing the stuffing by bringing the sides of the fish together with short skewers and lacing these together with thread.

Sweat

To draw out the juices from cut up vegetables over a gentle heat in a little melted fat. The vegetables can then be used as a base for braising meat, other whole vegetables or for preparing soup.

Sweating mixed sliced vegetables in melted fat in a lidded frying pan. Add chops or similar small pieces of meat for braising and complete the cooking in the same pan.

Tenderise

To break down the tough fibres in meat by beating it, marinating it (See MARINATE) or by sprinkling it with a proprietary brand of meat tenderiser.

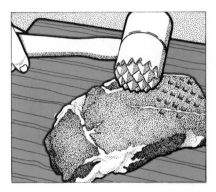

Beating a piece of steak prior to cooking with a special wooden meat hammer.

Thicken

To thicken the consistency of sauces, gravies and soups by adding flour blended with fat (see below) or cornflour blended with cold liquid, when a little hot sauce is added to the thickener, stirred and poured back into the sauce.

Sprinkling meat tenderiser on to a steak. Leave to stand at room temperature for about 30 minutes before cooking. Prick the surface of a roast all over before treating.

Adding beurre manié – a blended paste of flour and butter – to a stew to thicken the sauce. Add a small amount, whisk into the liquid and bring to the boil. Repeat until the sauce is thickened. (See page 7.)

Toss

To flip or turn food over lightly to coat with seasoning or dressing; or the traditional way of turning a pancake over.

1

Preparing to toss a pancake by sliding the mixture which has been cooked on one side to the edge of the pan.

2

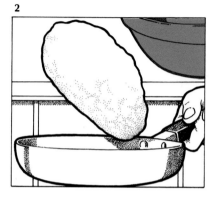

Tossing the pancake over with a sharp forward and back wrist action. Do not toss the pancake too high in the air.

Seasoning meat for a casserole by tossing it lightly in seasoned flour (see page 7) in a polythene bag. This ensures that every piece of meat is coated.

Tossing a salad in vinaigrette dressing in a bowl. Pour the correct amount of dressing into the bowl, then use servers to turn the salad over so that it is coated evenly.

Truss

To shape and secure poultry or joints of meat with string or skewers or both before cooking, to make it easier to carve. Any stuffing is added before trussing, which then holds the stuffing in place.

1

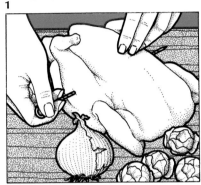

With chicken breast uppermost, pushing a skewer through the legs of a chicken, having bent the legs into position against the breast and pressed them well forward.

2

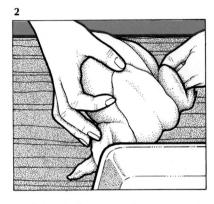

With the chicken breast downwards, pulling the neck flap of skin over to secure stuffing if used. Keep the wings splayed out at this stage.

3

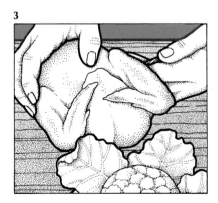

Twisting the wings and folding the tips over the neck flap of skin before securing with a skewer – through the fleshier part of one wing, across the bird's cavity and out through the other wing.

4

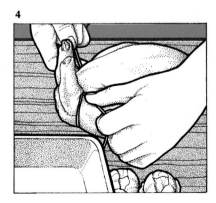

With the chicken breast uppermost, tying with string the legs and tail (parson's nose) neatly together.

Turn out

To remove food from the tin in which it has been cooked or the mould in which it has been set. Turned out food should hold its shape.

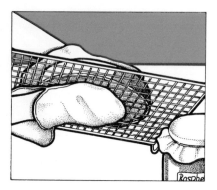

Inverting a Victoria sandwich cake on to a wire tray, while it is still hot but shrunken slightly away from the sides of the tin. This method leaves a lattice pattern on the cake. Turn the cake over after a few minutes.

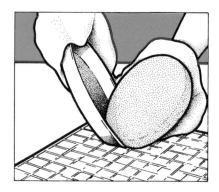

Turning out a sandwich cake to avoid the lattice pattern. Support the cake on the palm of the hand, covered with a cloth. Take care, for the cake will be fragile when hot.

Placing a loose bottomed flan tin on an upturned jar to make it easy to remove the flan intact. Pull the outer ring straight down to free the flan.

Lifting the oiled mould off a moulded rice salad. Pack the mould fairly tightly with the ingredients and chill thoroughly before turning it out.

Unmould

To remove foods intact from a specially shaped mould or container, in which they have been left to set or chill after cooking.

1

Sliding the tip of a round-bladed knife round the edge of a mould to loosen the sides of a jellied mixture.

2

Dipping the mould into a basin of hot water for just a few seconds in order to release the bottom of the set mixture. Dry the mould and put a wetted serving plate upside down on top.

3

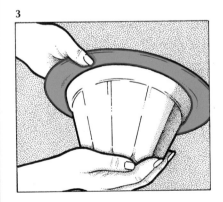

Inverting the plate and mould. Holding the mould on either side, shake gently to free the jelly. Place on the working surface and listen for mould's release.

4

Using both hands, lift the mould carefully off the jelly so as not to spoil its shape.

Whip

To beat a mixture or an ingredient until it is light and fluffy. Whipping increases the volume of a mixture by incorporating air. Use a fork, wire whisk, rotary or hand-held electric beater.

Using a fork to whip a *small* quantity of cream in order to avoid over whipping, which would make the cream too thick and buttery.

Whisk

To introduce air into egg whites to increase their volume, using a wire, rotary or electric whisk. Whisked egg whites should hold their shape.

Whisking egg whites with a wire whisk. Whisk vigorously and evenly throughout the mixture until stiff but not dry. When ready for use, the whites will stand up in glossy peaks.

Zest

To remove only the coloured part of the rind of citrus fruit. This part contains the oil that gives the characteristic flavour of the fruit – eg. orange, lemon or grapefruit.

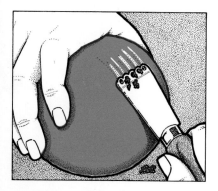

Using a zester – a small metal tool with a sharp claw edge and holes – to remove the zest from an orange.

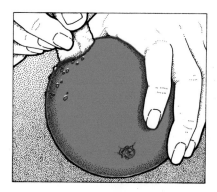

Rubbing the zest off an orange skin with a lump of sugar. Use this method for sweet dishes, when the zest-soaked sugar lump can be dissolved in the mixture.

Index

Almonds:
 Blanching 11
 Decorating with blanched
  almonds 29
 Flaking 34
 Paste decorations 29
 Slivers 81
 Toasted 29
American frosting, to spread
 37
Anchovy slivers 81
 Garnishing with 41
Angelica, to decorate with 29
Apples:
 Coating with fritter batter 22
 Coring 24
 Macerating dried 54
 Poached rings 60
 Pulped 64
Apricots:
 Jam glaze 42
 Macerating dried 54
 Puréed 65
 Snipping for stuffings 81
Arrowroot glaze 42
Asparagus:
 Scraping 71
 Steaming 83
Aubergines, to salt 68

Bacon:
 Barding with 10
 Larding with 50
 Lining terrines with 53
 Scoring 70
Baking powder, to measure 55
Batter, to beat 10
Beans:
 Blanching green 11
 Preserving runner beans in
  salt 63
 Refreshing green 65
Beef:
 Carving 17
 Larding 50
 Pressing spiced 63
Beurre manié 7, 89
Biscuits, to crush 26
Brandy, to flambé 35
Brandy snaps, to roll 67
Bread:
 Garnishes with 41
 Kneading dough 50
 Proving 64
 Rising 66
Butter:
 Clarifying 21
 Melting for pouring over
  pâtés 56
 Shaping pats, curls 41
Butter cream icing 46
Cabbage:
 Boiling 12
 Shredding 75
Cake tins, to line 51–2
Cakes:
 Baking two sandwich cakes 9
 Butter cream icing for 46
 Coating with nuts 22

Creaming 25
Decorating 27, 29
Dredging with icing sugar 31
Folding in flour 35
Glacé icing for 46, 47
Glazing with jam 42
Piped icing decorations 59
Rolling up a Swiss roll 68
Royal icing for 47
Rubbing in fat 68
Sifting flour for fatless
 sponges 76
Spreading with American
 frosting 37
Turning out 92
Carrot curls 40
Cauliflower, to steam 83
Celery:
 Slicing 80
 Tassels 40
Cheese, to grate 44
Cherries, to stone 85
Chicken:
 Boning 14
 Coating breasts with
  chaudfroid sauce 23
 Filleting 34
 Marinating 54
 Sautéeing joints 69
 Skinning 79
 Spit roasting 82
 Stuffing 87
 Trussing 91
Chives, to snip 81
Chocolate:
 Caraques 28
 Curls 28, 43
 Leaves 28
 Melted icing 47
 Melting 55
 Piping melted 27
Choux paste, piped 58
Cloves, to stud with 86
Crab, to dress 32
Cream:
 Scalding 69
 Whipping 94
Croûtons 41
Cucumber:
 Cones 39
 Crimping 25
 Deckle edged 39
Custard:
 Cups 84
 Sauce 12
 Tart 86

Dripping, scraping sediment off
 21
Dry brining 15
Duchesse potatoes, to pipe 59

Eggs:
 Binding with 11
 Boiling 12
 Coating with mayonnaise 23
 Folding whites into soufflé
  mixture 35
 Poaching 60
 Separating yolks and whites
  73–4

Shelling 74
Shirring 75
Slicing hard-boiled 80
Whisking whites 94

Fish. See also Herring etc:
 Boning 13
 Coating with batter 22
 Egg and breadcrumbing 23
 Filleting 33
 Flaking 34
 Frying fish cakes 38
 Gutting 45
 Marinating 54
 Masking 54
 Poaching 61
 Skewering 76
 Skinning 77–8
 Steaming 83
 Stuffed 88
Fritters:
 Deep frying 38
 Draining 31
Fruit. See also Apple etc:
 Paring 57
 Purée 62
 Scalding 69
 Seeding 72
 Stoning 85
Frying pan, to season a cast
 iron 71

Game, Game birds:
 Barding 10
 Drawing 31
 Hanging 45
 Larding 50
 Marinating 54
 Plucking 60
Gammon:
 Carving 16
 Snipping fat 82
 Sticking with cloves 86
Garlic, to crush 26
Gelatine, to dissolve 30
Gherkin fans 39
Glacé cherries, to decorate
 with 29
Glacé icing 46, 47
Glasses, to frost 37
Grapes:
 Decorating a Swiss roll with
  27
 Frosting 37
 Pipping 58
 Skinning 79
Grapefruit:
 Dividing into segments 73
 Shredding peel 75

Herring:
 Boning 13
 Crimping 25
 Sousing 82
Hot cross buns, to glaze 42

Jam, to skim scum off 77
Jelly bags, to scald 69
Jelly mixtures, to unmould 93

Kebabs 76

Kidney:
  Rendering fatty tissues 66
  Skinning and coring 24
Kipper, to pound for pâté 61

Lamb:
  Boning 13
  Carving 18
  Chining 20
  Skinning loin of 79
  Stewed 84
  Stuffed breast of 88
Lemon:
  Grating rind 43
  Twists and butterflies 39
Lettuce, to refresh 65
Lunch boxes, to freeze 36

Mackerel, to crimp 25
Meat. See also Beef etc:
  Barding 10
  Basting 10
  Batting 10
  Boning 13
  Braising 15
  Carving 16–18
  Chining 20
  Freezing chops 36
  Grilling chops 44
  Kebabs 76
  Larding 50
  Marinating 54
  Masking 54
  Mincing 56
  Pot roasting 61
  Pressing 63
  Rendering fatty trimmings 66
  Roasting 66–7
  Sealing 71
  Searing 71
  Seasoning a casserole 90
  Spit roasting 82
  Tenderising 89
Milk:
  Infusing for béchamel sauce 48
  Scalding 69
Mushrooms, 'turned' 40

Nutmeg, to grate 43
Nuts, to shell 74

Oil, to strain for re-use 85
Omelette, to brand 15
Onion:
  Chopping 20
  Dicing 30
  Rings 80
  Sticking with cloves 86
Orange:
  Dividing into segments 72
  Paring rind 57
  Peeling 57, 72
  Removing zest 94
  Shredding peel 75

Pan juices, to reduce 65

Pancakes:
  Frying 38
  Tossing 90
Parsley:
  Chopping 21
  Stirring into white sauce 85
Pastry:
  Baking blind 9
  Crimping 25
  Kneading 49
  Knocking up 50
  Lattice designs with 51
  Lining pudding basins with suet 53
  Mixing dough 56
  Rolling out 67
  Rubbing in fat 68
  Scalloping 70
  Sealing 71
  To decorate with 27
Peaches, to stone 85
Peppercorns, to grind 44
Peppers:
  Seeding 72
  Stuffing 87
Pheasant, to bard 10
Pig's trotters, to scald 69
Pineapple, to core 24
Pizzas, to garnish 41
Pork:
  Carving 18
  Chining 20
  Dry salt brine for 15
  Larding with 50
  Scalding 69
  Scoring 70
Potato:
  Deep frying chips 38
  Dicing 30
  Grating parboiled 43
  Parboiling 57
  Piping duchesse mixture 59
  Sieving 75
  Steaming 83
Poultry. See also Chicken etc:
  Barding 10
  Boning 14
  Carving 19
  Drawing 31
  Jointing 48–9
  Plucking 60
  Trussing 91
Prawns, to peel 57
Prunes, to macerate dried 54
Puddings:
  Boiling a suet 12
  Creaming 25
  Lining and covering basins with suet pastry 53
  Steaming 84

Radish roses etc. 39
Redcurrants:
  Frosting 28, 37
  Stringing 86
Risotto, simmering rice for 76
Royal icing 47
Runner beans, to salt 63

Salad, to toss 90
Salmon, to skin 77
Sauce:
  Seasoning a white 72
  Testing consistency of a coating 22
  Thickening 89
Sausage rolls, to slash tops of 79
Scones:
  Glazing 42
  Kneading dough 49
Shortbread:
  Rolling out mixture 67
  Scoring 70
Sole:
  Coating with chaudfroid sauce 23
  Skinning 78
Soups, to thicken 12
  Garnishing 41
Spices:
  Crushing 26
  Infusing for punch 48
Spring onion tassels 40
Steak, to brand 15
  Tenderising 89
Stews:
  Freezing in preformed packs 61–2
  Thickening 89
Strawberries:
  Freezing 36
  Hulling 45
Stuffing, to bind 11
Suet pudding, to boil 12
Sugar, to caramelise 16
Swiss roll, to roll up 68

Terrine, to line 53
Testing the set (jam-making) 62
Tomato:
  Skinning 78
  Slicing 80
  Waterlilies 40
  With hard-boiled egg 40
Tongue, pressed 63
Turkey:
  Carving 19
  Jointing 48–9

Veal:
  Batting 10
  Chining 20
Vegetables. See also Asparagus etc:
  Draining 31
  Puréed 64
  Seeding 72
  Sweating 89

Wet brining 16

Yeast, to froth 37